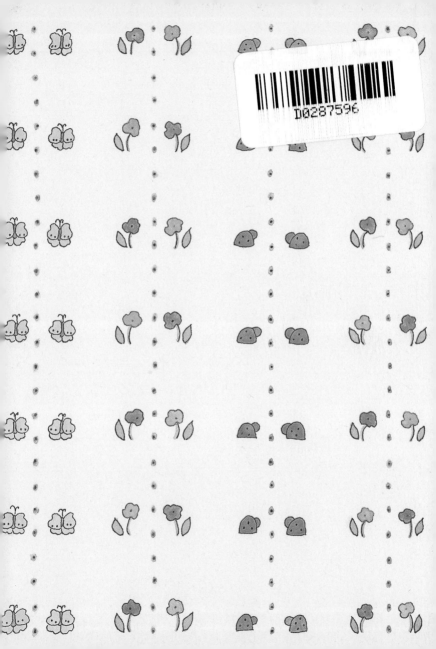

To:

From:

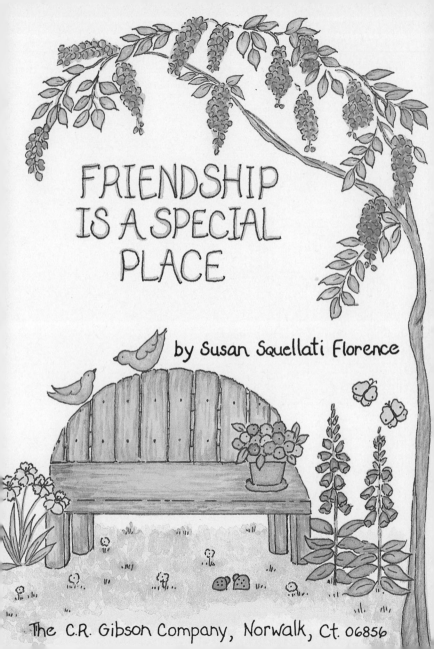

FRIENDSHIP IS A SPECIAL PLACE

by Susan Squellati Florence

The C.R. Gibson Company, Norwalk, Ct. 06856

Friendship
is a special place
untouched by time
or distance...

where feelings are felt
and thoughts are shared
with
someone
special.

Friendship
gives to heart
and soul
a voice

that is heard
in complete trust
and understanding.

True friends
come into our lives
at special times
and stay.

We travel separate journeys
and cross different bridges
with each other's help
and with the wonderful feeling
that we are not alone.

Friends become
our chosen family.
The ties are spun
with love and care.

Through our friends
we come to know
other families...

and learn of the different experiences that affect each other's lives.

Because of this we learn something precious and great...

In our joys
and our problems...
in our dreams
and our work...

we are all different.

And yet we feel
each other's special
place of caring within...

and we know
that we are all the same

The most magical part
of friendship is that
I can be who I am...
and you can be who you are...
totally.

Together,
we can laugh
in the midst
of a problem...

and find hope
in the midst
of despair.

By just being ourselves,
we help each other.

You can always
return to a friend
and find the same
warm feeling.

And whether we are together
or far apart ...
friendship will hold us
in its heart.

Friendship
is a special place...

I'm glad
we're there.

By Susan Squellati Florence

Friendship Is A Special Place
Babies Take Us On A Special Journey
A Book Of Loving Thoughts
A Gift Of Time
Your Journey
With Friends
The Heart Of Christmas
Hope Is Real